BABY SHOWERS

BABY SHOWERS

IDEAS & RECIPES FOR THE PERFECT PARTY

by gia russo and michele adams   photographs by jonelle weaver

CHRONICLE BOOKS

SAN FRANCISCO

Library of Congress Cataloging-in-Publication Data:

Adams, Michele.
Baby showers : ideas and recipes for the perfect party / by Michele Adams and
Gia Russo ; photographs by Jonelle Weaver.
p. cm.
ISBN 0-8118-2678-3 (pb)
1. Showers (Parties). 2. Infants. I. Russo, Gia. II. Title.
GV1472.7.S35A32   2000
792.3—dc21   99-37291
                                                            CIP

Printed in Hong Kong.

Prop styling by Michele Adams and Gia Russo
Food styling by Kimberly Huson
Designed by Sara Schneider

The photographer would like to thank Andy Kitchen for his assistance,
and Eric Tucker Photography for use of his studio. An additional thanks
to Kimberly, Mary Beth, and Rhonda for their awesome food styling.

Distributed in Canada by Raincoast Books
9050 Shaughnessy Street
Vancouver, British Columbia V6P 6E5

10 9 8 7 6 5 4 3 2 1

Chronicle Books LLC
85 Second Street
San Francisco, California 94105
www.chroniclebooks.com

DEDICATION

To my husband, Michael, for always being there to love me, support me, and make me laugh. I love you. To my Mom, for making me all that I am, and to my Dad, for giving me the courage to reach for my dreams. —Gia

To my husband, John, for his love and our future together. To my incredible parents, who have always believed in me and taught me the true meaning of family. And to my sweetest inspiration, Samuel James. —Michele

ACKNOWLEDGMENTS

It is with deep gratitude and appreciation that we acknowledge all of the people who helped make our dream a reality. Thanks to their cooperation and advice, our work on *Baby Showers* was both a successful and pleasurable experience.

Foremost on our list we would like to thank our editor, Mikyla Bruder, for her endless support and guidance; Sara Schneider for her amazing design skills, our photographer, Jonelle Weaver, for capturing our ideas so beautifully; and our food stylist, Kimberly Huson, for her remarkable talent and tireless efforts.

Among the others to whom we owe thanks are Stephen Breimer, for his sage advice; Amanda Adams, for her skilled hands; Jacqueline and John Adams, for graciously allowing us to shoot at their home; Elaine Auerbach, for being there when we needed a favor; Shannon Dilbeck, for her wonderful quilt work; Lorie Gianulli, for kindly loaning us her beautiful home; Jami Heidegger, for supplying us with all of her wonderful Kiehl's beauty products; and Eric Tucker, who generously provided us with access to his studio.

A baby shower is a memorable and practical occasion—a time for friends and family to come together in celebration of the imminent arrival of a new life, and an opportunity to provide the expectant mother (or couple) with many of the items necessary to care for a newborn. It has long been customary for a family member or close friend to throw the baby shower. Today, it is common for men to be included in the celebration. If you decide to throw a shower for a loved one, you will no doubt want to plan a thoughtful and fitting tribute to this momentous occasion. *Baby Showers* is meant to give you a starting point for this endeavor.

The baby shower is a uniquely American tradition. The birth of a child is celebrated throughout the world in many different ways. In most cultures it is customary to celebrate after the child is born. Traditional African cultures observe "life-cycle" ceremonies, including a "seclusion" ceremony, in which the mother and baby (and sometimes the father) are secluded from the community for a period of days following birth, and a naming ceremony, in which the child is named and introduced to the community. European Christians throw a party when a baby is christened, giving friends and family an opportunity to shower the baby with gifts (money, silver, and gold items) and to drink to the baby's good health.

Other cultures, however, do practice pre-birth rites and ceremonies. There are many pre-birth traditions related to Shinto, the ancient native religion of Japan. Most commonly, families will go to shrines to pray for a healthy baby and to purchase charms while the mother is pregnant. Perhaps closest to the American tradition of baby showers is the

Navajo practice of "Blessingways." The participants in a Blessingway often begin by pampering the mother-to-be: washing her feet in rose water, brushing her hair, bringing her tea, and lighting candles. Soon the blessings begin, and each guest expresses his or her love for the expectant mother and wishes for her and her newborn. This tradition of honoring the mother inspired our "Luncheon for Mom" shower in Chapter Three.

The origins and history of baby showers in America is difficult to trace. They may have begun in the 1920s, with Italian-Americans who believed in giving the mother-to-be a crib in anticipation of the arrival of a new baby. Some have called the tradition of baby showers a "Hallmark" creation—an excuse to spend money on cards and gifts. However, we believe that the baby shower is an occasion derived from the rich traditions of the many peoples and cultures that make up the United States. It is a natural human desire to provide a new mother and child with a head start and mark the milestone with warm sentiments.

The ideas in *Baby Showers* were inspired by both our personal and professional experiences. The many showers that we have attended or hosted provided an abundant source of inspiration. The "Daisy Brunch" was inspired by a shower thrown by Michele. Against the backdrop of a warm spring morning, she created a charming shower where the gifts were kept simple, close friends brought items for the buffet, and each guest received a small paper box filled with cookies and trimmed with a fresh daisy as a favor. "Decorating the Nursery" grew out of our desire to create a fun coed shower that allows close family and friends to share in the excitement of preparing the nursery for the arrival of the baby. "Luncheon for Mom" mixes the Navajo practice of Blessingways with a traditional American shower.

As freelance stylists and as editors for *Martha Stewart Living*, we have learned the significance of themes, palettes, beauty, and simplicity. But above all, we place great importance on the organization and planning of an event. Chapter One, "The Baby Shower," offers a general framework that will help you to plan and prepare for your shower. Each party chapter presents a section called "Putting It Together," which gives more specific information on how to get organized.

The parties in *Baby Showers* can be easily re-created or adapted to meet your personal needs. You will find a variety of styles, from the traditional "Luncheon for Mom" set in the cool shade of a backyard garden to the more casual coed "Decorating the Nursery" party. You will also find a variety of menus, decorations, and locations that can be modified depending upon where you live. You'll want to select the shower whose theme best suits your needs. It has been our experience that the most successful showers have a theme that reflects the spirit of the mother or the couple. Each of the showers we offer here has its own unique theme, and in many ways, deciding upon the theme makes the task of the host much easier. Themes set the mood, determine the guest list, influence the menu, suggest gifts, and bring focus to the guest (or guests) of honor.

Above all, our intention in *Baby Showers* is to inspire you. There is no better way to make loved ones feel special than to put real thought and energy into creating a party just for them. We hope the ideas in this book will make your job a little easier and help you to host an unforgettable shower for someone you love.

THE BABY SHOWER

PARTY PLANNING

Once you have decided to host a baby shower, you will need to do some preliminary planning. There are a few overriding issues you should consider first: possible themes, possible locations, and guest list. Choose a date that is one month to two months before the delivery (this allows for the baby coming earlier than his or her due date). As you make the big decisions, keep in mind that this celebration should reflect the personality and spirit of the mother or couple. Also, don't forget to review practical items such as when and where the party will take place, who's on the guest list, and how weather might affect the location. Once you've worked out these issues, you're ready to tackle some of the finer points: invitations, menu, decorations, favors, gifts, and how to prepare and organize it all.

CHOOSING A THEME

Choosing a theme is the best possible way to kick-start your planning. A theme gives immediate direction to your celebration and helps to determine the guest list, the decor, the palette, the menu, the favors, and the gifts. In this book we present four themes that you may elect to follow or simply use for inspiration. You don't need to fret over choosing the most elaborate theme; remember that a theme can be as simple as a type of fruit, a season of the year, or even a color. Just remember to keep your guest (or guests) of honor—the focus of the celebration—in mind as you choose your theme.

THE LOCATION

The location you select will have a direct effect on many factors, foremost of which is the size of your guest list. For some people, the selection of a beautiful location is more important than the number of guests it will accommodate. Others prefer to know how many guests they'll be entertaining before choosing a location. No matter which side of the equation you fall on, remember that you needn't limit yourself to the obvious spaces. If the weather is good, a garden, terrace, or even park or beach would make an excellent location for a large gathering. Your home or garden may be the ideal choice. You have constant access, and no limit to the time you can take for preparation. When you look at your home with a renewed purpose, you will find many possibilities. Set up a buffet in your dining room or even a hallway. Remove extra furniture from the room you'll be using so that your party decorations won't compete with their surroundings. Whether you've decided to have the shower indoors or out, the fact that there will be people coming to your house will most likely spur you into action. It's not the time to take on a remodeling project; simply focus on cleaning the areas where guests will be. Don't forget the bathroom. A stack of clean hand towels, fresh soaps, and an extra roll of toilet paper will be appreciated. Tidy up the garden and entry area, repotting containers with blooming plants, if necessary.

THE GUESTS

Once you've decided upon your theme and location, you'll have a good sense of the number of guests you'll want to invite. The showers in this book can be adapted for intimate parties, as well as large gatherings. However, there are several factors that will help to determine the size of your guest list: the number of friends and family in the area, your budget, the amount of time you have to prepare, the size of the location, and whether or not this is the first baby born to the family. Unless the shower is a surprise, remember to consult the mother-to-be to confirm who should be invited.

INVITATIONS

The invitation is your first opportunity to present your guests with the shower's theme. An invitation that is thoughtfully selected or carefully designed will build anticipation for the event. With so many choices of paper and materials your options are numerous.

Invitations should go out four weeks in advance and should include an RSVP date and a phone number. Your RSVP date should give guests approximately two weeks to respond to the invitation unless you're on a tight schedule. Be sure to factor in enough time up front for gathering the address list, making and addressing the invitations, and delivery.

Spend some time browsing your local art or paper store when you go to purchase the supplies needed to make an invitation. Look for unusual rubber stamps or craft cutouts in different shapes and sizes. Sort through the wide array of paper available, but keep in mind that not all papers will work for every method of printing. Handmade cards don't need to be complicated. In "Decorating the Nursery," we opted for a basic white note card and added cut paint chips to decorate the cover so the theme would be apparent to the guests. Small details—small buttons glued at the top of the card or a ribbon trimming glued along the edges—can turn a simple card into a true standout.

THE MENU

In planning these menus we selected foods that taste great, look beautiful, and are easy to prepare. Since every shower is designed around a theme, menus are chosen to complement the setting and mood. For example, the light citrus-flavored foods for "Heirlooms and

Memories" reflect the citrus theme. A hearty picnic for "Decorating the Nursery" satisfies your guests and energizes them for the day's work. Although each menu has been developed for a specific number of people, it can be tailored to fit your needs and adjusted to the size and season of the shower.

Because preparing the food is one of the most time-consuming tasks of entertaining, we've selected recipes that are easy to prepare and many that can be made in advance. The menus we've chosen for the showers in this book can be handled alone, but consider asking a friend or two for help with the preparation. Delegating some of the work to a friend takes some of the pressure off you, and your friend may appreciate being involved. The "Putting It Together" section at the beginning of each chapter will help you manage your time and keep the process moving smoothly.

THE AMBIENCE

This is the fun part—the opportunity to flex your creative muscles as you transform the location with all of the elements you've selected. The way you choose to decorate will have the greatest effect on the mood or ambience of the shower. The impression your guests have as they walk into the shower setting will be the direct result of the choices you make with respect to color, materials, serving pieces, and food presentation.

Begin the decorating process by drawing inspiration from your theme, menu, or location. The decorating style chosen for each of the showers in this book developed in a different way. In the case of the "Daisy Brunch," the daisy theme served as inspiration for the decorating. In the "Heirlooms and Memories" shower, the citrus menu was reflected in the decor. As you conceive how to decorate your location, you should also keep in mind the personality of the guest of honor and the formality of the party.

Color is another simple way to evoke a mood, and we suggest developing a palette for the party early on. In our "Luncheon for Mom" shower, pink gingham linens accented with pale green create a distinctly feminine feel. In the "Decorating the Nursery" shower, a palette of blues and white was designed with the coed guest list in mind. Try experimenting with colors normally overlooked for a shower. Your local paint store is a great source for color ideas—manufacturers provide a wealth of possible combinations, especially in neutrals and pastels, which are good accents for wood, stone, and metal.

As you gather decorations for your shower, remember that the party doesn't need to be expensive to be a success. You can find all the components for the parties in this book at your local discount craft and import stores. Yards of blue-and-white ticking stripe are inexpensive, and draped as a canopy this material can transform the setting. A simple arrangement of citrus fruit from the grocery store or farmers' market can become a striking centerpiece. As you begin to decorate your location, keep in mind the guiding principles of beauty, simplicity, and practicality. You want to create an environment that is impressive but not intrusive. Centerpieces should be kept low to allow guests to see across their tables, decorations strung from the ceiling should be kept above head height, and tables and furniture should be spaced with plenty of room for free movement. With just a little thought and planning you can create an ambience that will leave a lasting impression.

Presenting favors is the perfect way to thank your guests and provide them with a wonderful remembrance of the shower. For "Heirlooms and Memories," we pulled the citrus theme into the favor by making citrus-shaped marzipan fruits, wrapped in melon-colored netting and tied with green floral wire. A wood tray placed adjacent to the door offered neat rows of the delicate favors to guests as they said goodbye.

Favors should always be individually packaged and portable. Designing this packaging presents yet another great opportunity to express your creativity. Small treats like chocolates, cookies, nuts, and candies are inexpensive and easy to package. For a unique twist consider using Chinese takeout containers, translucent cellophane bags, delicate wooden boxes, or small metal tins. Finished with colorful ribbon, sprigs of leaves, or fresh flowers, favors become special decorations for the shower, as well as gifts for the guests.

THE GIFTS

As you plan your shower you'll want to make accommodations for the gift-giving ceremony. Start by considering where the gifts will be placed as the guests arrive. The way you present the gifts can add beauty to your location and a sense of excitement. You'll also want to allot a sufficient amount of time during the shower for the opening of the gifts. If you rush the gift ceremony, you'll deny one of the best opportunities for the mother-to-be to interact with her guests. Finally, be sure to provide an intimate setting for the gift giving—one that allows the mother-to-be to see and acknowledge all of her guests and allows every guest a clear view of the expectant mother during the special moment.

Of course, one of the most difficult aspects of gift giving is deciding exactly what to give. A good way to begin the decision process is by checking the mother's registry (if she is registered) to find out exactly what she needs. Or, you might start by considering the necessities of every baby—a crib, stroller, car seat, linens, onesies, booties, etc. Be sure not to overlook your own talents as you decide what to give. We have always been inspired by handmade gifts and we believe that they are especially appropriate for a shower. A knitted sweater, a quilted blanket, or a handcrafted cradle is the sincerest gift of all.

Whether you make the gift yourself or select a store-bought item, spend some time making the package just as beautiful as your intentions. Try solid-colored or simple-patterned papers and tissues. Experiment with ribbons in satin, velvet, grosgrain, and silk as well as other delicate trimmings. Tie fresh or silk flowers into the bow for a quick and beautiful embellishment. If possible, wrap your gift in accordance with the shower's theme. For the "Daisy Brunch," we glued small daisies to a white box wrapped with a yellow bow.

GETTING ORGANIZED

Throwing a shower can overwhelm even the most organized person, but you can alleviate a lot of the stress by starting early with a good plan. Our "Party Planner" (page 21) provides some specific guidelines for getting organized, but there are other areas you'll need to consider in order to maintain control and reduce anxiety before and during the shower.

Once you've made all the practical decisions about the theme, location, guests, invitations, menu, decorations, favors, and gifts, you'll need to figure out exactly what needs to be done and when you're going to do it. Begin right away by making a master list of everything you'll need to do to pull off the shower. Then figure out how much time you'll need to accomplish each item on your list and organize those items into a time schedule. The time schedule is invaluable—it will prevent you from pushing everything to the last minute or underestimating how much time you really need.

Making a master list is also a good way to begin creating shopping lists. Compile shopping lists as soon as you can, and organize them by the type of store you're going to be visiting—grocery, craft, fabric, hardware. These lists will help save time by preventing extra trips to the store, especially during the critical few days before the shower. It's a good idea to keep them with you in case you have a free moment to pick up a few items. Just remember, the more you can put down on paper, the more control you'll feel you have, and the fewer small but important things (like napkins or garnishes for drinks) will be forgotten.

Try to get as much of your shopping as possible out of the way early on. Purchase the non-perishable items you need for invitations, decorating, and favors right away, and shop for or make your gift a few weeks in advance. Wrap your gift ahead of time and you won't have to worry about it again. If your favors can be made in advance, get them done as well. With those details taken care of, you will be free to concentrate on decorating the location and preparing the food in the few days before the shower.

Many of the recipes in this book have been designed for preparation ahead of time, so be sure to scan each recipe to note how far in advance it can be made (you will find specific menu preparation information for each shower in the following chapters). Once you know how long each item will take to make, create a food preparation schedule that details what needs to be made on which day. If you plan to have the help of friends or relatives, coordinate this schedule with them. As for the food shopping, the items you'll need can be grouped into three easy lists: kitchen and baking supplies, groceries for the week in advance, and groceries for a day or two before the shower.

If the shower is being thrown in your home, set aside some time a week or two before the event to clean and organize your house or yard—this will free your time for last-minute preparation. During this time you'll want to gather and set aside the household materials you'll be using for the party. Wash and iron the linens, if necessary, and set them aside where they won't be disturbed. Wash and polish serving pieces like platters, vases for flower arrangements, candleholders, plates, and silverware. Label each serving piece with the menu item it will hold. Then do a practice setting of the table or buffet to confirm that your choices work together. This gives you a chance to make any changes in your plan, or to note any additional items that you will need.

The most important thing to remember is that throwing a shower is supposed to be fun. Try using our Party Planner, and adapt it to your needs. Making the lists and creating the schedules may seem like more work, but you will appreciate having done it in the end. The more organizing you do up front, the more enjoyable the process will be. And, it is a general rule that if the host is having fun, chances are the guests will have fun too. So plan rigorously, and enjoy the party.

SIX OR MORE WEEKS AHEAD

Speak with the mother-to-be about basic decisions of date,
  location, time of day, guest list, theme, and style of shower
Make master "to do" planning list

FOUR TO SIX WEEKS AHEAD

Gather address list of guests
Shop for or make invitations
Choose menu
Place order for any rental equipment
Shop for or make gift for mom or baby

THREE TO FOUR WEEKS AHEAD

Send out invitations
Shop for decorations and any special serving pieces, supplies,
  or equipment
Work on special decorations like tablecloths and favors

TWO TO THREE WEEKS AHEAD

Gather and clean serving pieces, table linens, and tableware,
  and clean and store them in a convenient place
Make shopping lists for recipe ingredients
Place flower order

ONE TO TWO WEEKS AHEAD

Wrap shower gift
Begin cleaning house and/or yard

FIVE TO SEVEN DAYS AHEAD

Shop for recipe ingredients
Begin setting up for party
Confirm order and delivery time for rentals and flowers
Finish any last-minute decorations
Finish cleaning party location
Confirm RSVPs

1 ② 3 4 5

DAISY BRUNCH

DECORATIONS AND GIFT IDEAS

    DAISY INVITATIONS

    TRIMMED CLOTHING AND BATH SET

MENU

    YELLOW PEPPER FRITTATA

    SMOKED SALMON BITES

    BLUEBERRY BISCUITS WITH SMOKED TURKEY

        AND BLUEBERRY CHUTNEY

    INDIVIDUAL QUICHES

    BLANCHED ASPARAGUS WITH LEMON-DILL

        DIPPING SAUCE

    HONEY-BAKED HAM

    FRENCH TOAST WITH MASCARPONE AND

        SUGARED BERRIES

    SLICED MELONS AND BERRIES WITH MINTED

        HONEY-LIME DRESSING

    GLAZED LEMON BUNDT CAKE

    ORANGE JUICE

    COFFEE / TEA

Throughout the ages, flowers have been used to symbolize human qualities and emotions. No flower better inspires the celebration and anticipation of a new life than the white daisy, the age-old symbol of innocence and purity. In our Daisy Brunch, a gentle garden setting is perfect for a late-morning meal permeated by the daisy theme. A palette of yellow and white, a menu of sweet and savory flavors, and a buffet brimming with daisies create an ambience that is both symbolic and unforgettable.

Daisies are commonly associated with spring and summer, and a garden setting in the late spring or early summer is a natural choice for this colorful brunch. If you don't have access to a garden, you can still pull the essence of spring into the space you have selected. Draw back the curtains to allow the morning light to wash over the room; decorate the room with vases full of daisies; light an aromatic candle to fill the air with the fragrance of jasmine or gardenia.

The handmade Daisy Invitations, which can easily be fabricated from basic craft supplies, will signal the theme of the special event. Like all handmade items, though, this invitation will require extra time and devotion. Be sure to plan accordingly to allow time for making and mailing your invitations.

In designing the menu for the Daisy Brunch, we selected items with the contrasting flavors of sweet and savory. French Toast with Mascarpone and Sugared Berries is offset by the pungent flavor of Yellow Pepper Frittata; sweet Blueberry Biscuits are combined with sliced Smoked Turkey and Blueberry Chutney. A honey-baked ham can be ordered in advance from your grocery store. With these and the other recipes presented in this chapter, you are sure to have something to please everyone.

All the hours spent planning and preparing for the Daisy Brunch are rewarded during the decorating phase. We began our decorating by designing the focal point of the shower—the buffet. We draped square tables with white linens and placed them against the backdrop of the garden. Each of the tables was covered with a bed of fresh daisy heads. Tiered serving pieces and cake stands of varying heights rose from the bed of daisies to present the food in a tantalizing display. Each of the three tables presented a different type of food: sweet, savory, and egg entrees.

Guest tables were covered with soft yellow linens. In the center of the round tables we placed fresh-cut daisies in painted white pots. Since all of the plates had been stacked on the buffet table, we filled the void between place settings with the favors, yellow gumdrops in cellophane bags. We tied each bag with yellow rickrack and glued a daisy appliqué to the center of the rickrack streamers. Conveniently adjacent to the guest tables we set up a drink table brimming with freshly squeezed orange juice, coffee, tea, and water.

At the end of the buffet we placed the gift table. For this shower, we wrapped gifts in shades of green, blue, yellow, or white, and most incorporated daisies in some way. While it's impossible to expect all of your guests to wrap their gifts in such a fashion, we have included these ideas as inspiration for those who wish to go the extra mile.

As a final gesture to the mother-to-be on her special day, we recommend handmade gifts. For this chapter we created a gift idea that is simple and endearing. The project is no more complicated than sewing a trimming or appliqué to the basic items all babies require—T-shirts, onesies, hooded towels, washcloths, and booties. All of the items needed for these gifts are readily available and inexpensive.

PUTTING IT TOGETHER

FOUR WEEKS AHEAD

Make and send out Daisy Invitations

Make and wrap gift

THREE OR FOUR DAYS AHEAD

Purchase groceries and order honey-baked ham

Make Blueberry Chutney

Make Mascarpone cream cheese for French Toast

Dice prosciutto and shred cheese for Quiches

TWO DAYS AHEAD

Receive and set up rentals

Set out table linens; touch up with iron if needed

Pick up daisies for centerpieces and buffet tables

Bake Blueberry Biscuits and phyllo cups for Salmon Bites

Make Lemon-Dill Dipping Sauce for Blanched Asparagus

Purchase fresh smoked turkey for Blueberry Biscuits

ONE DAY BEFORE

Bake Individual Quiches

Soak French Toast slices

Blanch asparagus and refrigerate overnight

Slice melons and make Minted Honey-Lime Dressing (keep separate)

Bake Glazed Lemon Bundt Cake; slice lemons for syrup

Slice vegetables and shred cheese for Frittata

THE MORNING OF THE SHOWER

Make centerpieces and place on guest tables

Bake Yellow Pepper Frittata

Finish prepping and assembling Smoked Salmon Bites

Assemble Blueberry Biscuits with Smoked Turkey

Make Sugared Berries and cook French Toast

JUST BEFORE THE SHOWER

Decorate buffet tables with daisy heads

Reheat Quiches and make Lemon Bundt Cake syrup

Make coffee and tea and set out food and beverages

PLEASE JOIN US FOR A
"DAISY" BRUNCH

DAISY INVITATIONS

The perfect way to begin a daisy theme shower is with this daisy invitation. This simple card requires only basic craft supplies. If you're planning to invite more than 12 guests, you may want to enlist the help of a couple of friends, especially someone with great handwriting.

WHITE AND YELLOW CARD STOCK

SCISSORS

GLUE STICK

CRAFT GLUE

1-INCH YELLOW POMPOMS

BLUE OR GREEN FELT-TIP PEN (FINE)

8-BY-8-INCH WHITE ENVELOPES

Sketch your own 7-inch daisy template on the back of the card stock. Be sure to make the petals wide enough for you to write all of the shower information on them. Cut out your daisy template and lightly trace it onto the back of the card stock. If you're creating 12 invitations, you'll need to trace it 12 times onto both the yellow and white stock. Cut out all of the daisies.

Take a white daisy and apply glue stick to the back. Place the white daisy on top of a yellow daisy and rotate it slightly to offset the two. Using the craft glue, adhere the pompom to the center of the white daisy. Allow all of your invitations to dry for 30 minutes before personalizing them with the felt-tip pen. Remember to address your envelopes before placing the invitation inside. Once you place the daisy inside the envelope, the pompom will create a small bump that makes writing impossible.

TRIMMED CLOTHING AND BATH SET

You can find plain white cotton baby basics at discount or department stores. Make them special by embellishing them with trimmings from the fabric shop. Trim the front of a onesie, the cuff of a baby sock, or the edge of a little cap.

TRIMMING (LENGTH WILL VARY FOR
  EACH PIECE—MEASURE WHAT YOU
  WILL NEED BEFORE YOU BEGIN)
  SUCH AS RICKRACK, RIBBON, AND
  SEAM BINDING

STRAIGHT PINS

MEDIUM-POINT NEEDLE AND
  MATCHING THREAD OR A SEWING
  MACHINE

WHITE COTTON BABY BASICS SUCH AS
  ONESIES, T-SHIRTS, WRAP SHIRTS,
  PAJAMA SETS, HOODED TOWEL
  WASHCLOTH SETS, RECEIVING
  BLANKETS, CAPS, BOOTIES, AND
  SOCKS

Place trimming on the desired area of the clothing or linens and secure with straight pins. Use your imagination! With a sewing machine or by hand, stitch the trimming to the cloth to secure. Be sure to stitch it on securely so the baby can't pull it off.

YELLOW PEPPER FRITTATA

Try serving tiny squares of frittata on toasted baguette slices, topped with a favorite chutney. Prep vegetables and cheese and store in the refrigerator the day before the party so frittata can be quickly made the morning of the shower.

---

2 TABLESPOONS OLIVE OIL

2 TABLESPOONS BUTTER

3 ONIONS, SLICED

3 YELLOW PEPPERS, SLICED INTO
    SLIVERS

18 EGGS

2 CUPS HALF-AND-HALF OR
    WHOLE MILK

CRACKED BLACK PEPPER

2 CUPS GRATED CHEDDAR OR
    GRUYÈRE CHEESE

TWO 14-OUNCE CANS ARTICHOKE
    HEARTS (IN WATER), DRAINED

2 TABLESPOONS THYME LEAVES

1 TABLESPOON CHOPPED SAGE LEAVES

Preheat oven to 350° F. Prepare a 9-by-12-inch baking dish with nonstick spray. Warm the olive oil and butter in a large nonstick frying pan over medium-low heat until the butter has melted. Add the onions and cook, stirring occasionally, for about 15 minutes, or until onions are soft and golden brown. Add the peppers and continue cooking until soft (about 10 minutes); remove from heat. In a large bowl, crack the eggs and add the half-and-half and black pepper; whisk to combine. In another large bowl, add the onions, peppers, cheese, artichoke hearts, and herbs, and toss to combine. Spread the vegetable mixture into the prepared baking dish, pouring the egg mixture over, and bake about 40 minutes, until set. Remove from oven and let cool slightly. Slice into squares with a serrated knife. Keep warm in oven on the lowest temperature setting until ready to serve.

Serves 30.

SMOKED SALMON BITES

Mini muffin tins are the perfect size to shape the delicate phyllo cups. Make phyllo cups up to two days in advance, and leave time the morning of the shower to arrange ingredients in the cups.

---

1 PACKAGE PHYLLO DOUGH

6 TABLESPOONS BUTTER, MELTED

8 OUNCES CRÈME FRAÎCHE OR
    SOUR CREAM

8 OUNCES SMOKED SALMON

4 OUNCES CAVIAR

1 LEMON, SLICED PAPER THIN

36 SMALL SPRIGS FRESH DILL

Preheat oven to 350° F. Unwrap the phyllo dough and place sheets under a damp towel while working to keep them from drying out. Place five stacked sheets of phyllo on a cutting board, and use a knife to cut lengthwise and crosswise into approximately 3-inch squares. Press three small sheets of phyllo into each tin cup and brush with butter. Place the remaining two sheets on top at a 45-degree angle; brush again with butter. Repeat until all tin cups are filled. Bake for 6 minutes, or until lightly golden (watch carefully, as phyllo browns quickly). Allow to cool and store in airtight containers or on a tray covered in plastic wrap. Fill each cup with 1 teaspoon of the crème fraîche and a small piece of salmon, and top with 1/4 teaspoon of the caviar. Cut each lemon slice into eighths. Garnish each cup with a piece of lemon and a small sprig of dill. Keep refrigerated until ready to serve.

Serves 36.

BLUEBERRY BISCUITS WITH SMOKED TURKEY

These little biscuits combine sweet and savory tastes in one bite. To save time, purchase the smoked
turkey from your favorite deli and have it sliced thin. Bake the biscuits two or three days ahead and assemble
the morning of the shower. Make the chutney three to four days ahead.

For the biscuits:

4 CUPS ALL-PURPOSE FLOUR

2 TABLESPOONS BAKING POWDER

1 1/2 TEASPOONS SALT

6 TABLESPOONS SUGAR

2 TABLESPOONS GRATED LEMON ZEST

4 TABLESPOONS UNSALTED BUTTER,
    CHILLED AND CUT INTO PIECES

2 CUPS BUTTERMILK

1 BASKET FRESH BLUEBERRIES, RINSED
    AND DRAINED, OR 1 PINT FROZEN
    BLUEBERRIES, THAWED AND
    DRAINED

1/2 POUND SMOKED TURKEY, SLICED

To make the biscuits, first preheat oven to 400° F. Spray a baking sheet with nonstick cooking spray. In a large bowl, whisk together the first five ingredients until well blended. With a pastry blender or your fingers, cut in the butter until the mixture resembles coarse meal. Using a fork, slowly stir in the buttermilk until the dough begins to hold together (you may not need to use all the buttermilk). Gently and gradually add the blueberries with your hands until incorporated. Do not overwork the dough, or the biscuits will be tough. Drop the dough by heaping tablespoons onto the baking sheet. Bake for 12 minutes, or until tops and bottoms begin to brown. Cool slightly and transfer to a wire rack. Store in an airtight container in the refrigerator up to three days, but bring to room temperature before assembling.

Makes 30 biscuits.

To assemble biscuits, slice with a serrated knife and fill with a few slices of smoked turkey and a dollop of Blueberry Chutney (page 38).

BLUEBERRY CHUTNEY

This flavorful chutney is a zesty blend of lemon, ginger, and blueberries—a perfect complement to the Blueberry Biscuits with Smoked Turkey (page 37). Make the chutney three to four days ahead and refrigerate until ready to serve.

$^1/_2$ CUP SUGAR

$^1/_4$ CUP LEMON JUICE, FRESHLY
    SQUEEZED

1 TABLESPOON FRESH GINGER,
    PEELED AND MINCED

$^1/_8$ TABLESPOON NUTMEG

2 BASKETS FRESH BLUEBERRIES,
    RINSED OR DRAINED, OR
    2 PINTS FROZEN BLUEBERRIES,
    THAWED AND DRAINED

$^1/_2$ CUP GOLDEN RAISINS

2 TABLESPOONS GRATED LEMON ZEST

$^1/_4$ CUP CHOPPED TOASTED ALMONDS

To make the chutney, combine the sugar, lemon juice, ginger, and nutmeg in a medium saucepan. Bring to a boil, stirring until sugar dissolves. Reduce heat and simmer for 5 minutes. Add 1 basket of the blueberries and the raisins. Cook until berries pop and juices thicken, stirring often. Add the remaining blueberries, the lemon zest, and almonds. Stir until just heated through. Allow to cool, and place in an airtight container in refrigerator. Serve cold or at room temperature.

Makes 2 cups.

INDIVIDUAL QUICHES

Making individual servings of quiche is an easy and beautiful way to serve your guests. Dice the prosciutto and shred the cheese three days before the shower. Bake the quiches the day before; store in the refrigerator and reheat before serving.

---

2 PACKAGES PREPARED PIE
    CRUST ROUNDS

9 EGGS

1 1/2 CUPS CREAM OR MILK

6 OUNCES PROSCIUTTO, DICED

6 OUNCES GRUYÈRE CHEESE,
    SHREDDED

CRACKED PEPPER TO TASTE

36 SPRIGS ITALIAN PARSLEY

Preheat oven to 350° F. Spray muffin tins with nonstick cooking spray. On a lightly floured surface, roll each pie crust round out to approximately 10 inches. Using a 3 1/2-inch round cutter (the rim of a cup or jar works equally well), cut several round pieces from each crust. Press leftover crust together, roll out again, and cut several more rounds. Repeat until you have 36 rounds. Place a round into each cup of the muffin tins, pressing with fingers to form a mini pie crust. In a large bowl, whisk the eggs and cream together. Place 1 teaspoon of the prosciutto and 2 tablespoons of the shredded Gruyère into each crust. Pour egg mixture into each crust until almost full and sprinkle with pepper. Place a sprig of Italian parsley on top of each quiche. Bake for 25 minutes or until crust is golden and eggs are set.

Serves 36.

BLANCHED ASPARAGUS WITH LEMON-DILL DIPPING SAUCE

Fresh, crisp stalks of asparagus are a wonderful complement to any brunch menu. Feel free to substitute with julienned carrots, haricot verts, or jicama sticks. The dipping sauce can be made two days ahead and the asparagus the day before.

For the blanched asparagus:

2 POUNDS ASPARAGUS, TRIMMED
    TO 4- TO 6-INCH LENGTHS

1 LARGE BOWL ICED WATER

For the dipping sauce:

1 CUP CRÈME FRAÎCHE

1/4 CUP LEMON JUICE

1 TABLESPOON LEMON ZEST

1/2 CUP CHOPPED FRESH DILL

2 SHALLOTS, FINELY CHOPPED

SALT AND PEPPER TO TASTE

To make the asparagus, boil water in a large open saucepan or frying pan. Place the asparagus in boiling water for about 3 minutes, until bright green and slightly crisp. Drain in a colander and immediately plunge into the bowl of iced water. When thoroughly cool, transfer to a tray lined with paper towels. Cover with plastic wrap and refrigerate until serving, or up to 1 day before the party.

Serves 30 (2 stalks each).

To make the dipping sauce, mix the crème fraîche, lemon juice, zest, dill, and shallots together using a wire whisk. Season to taste with salt and pepper. Chill in refrigerator at least 2 hours and up to 2 days before the party.

Makes 1 1/2 cups.

FRENCH TOAST WITH MASCARPONE
AND SUGARED BERRIES

Mascarpone is a rich yet mild double cream cheese from Italy. When paired with thick slices of French toast
and sugared berries, the result is pure heaven. Make the Mascarpone cream cheese up to three days ahead, start the
French toast the day before, and grill toasts and make sugared berries the morning of the shower.

---

16 OUNCES MASCARPONE CHEESE

$1/4$ CUP PLUS 3 TABLESPOONS SUGAR

$1/4$ CUP ORANGE JUICE CONCENTRATE

ZEST OF 1 ORANGE

2 BASKETS STRAWBERRIES, RINSED,
    HULLED, AND QUARTERED

12 EGGS

2 CUPS HALF-AND-HALF

2 TABLESPOONS VANILLA EXTRACT

2 TEASPOONS CINNAMON

3 BAGUETTES FRENCH BREAD, SLICED
    DIAGONALLY 1 INCH THICK

4 TABLESPOONS BUTTER

$1/4$ CUP BALSAMIC VINEGAR

Whisk the cheese, the 3 tablespoons of sugar, the orange juice concentrate, and zest together in a medium bowl. Cover and refrigerate until cool, or up to 3 days.

Combine the strawberries and the $1/4$ cup of sugar in a large bowl. Let stand, refrigerated, for $1/2$ hour.

Crack the eggs into a large bowl, adding the half-and-half, vanilla, and cinnamon. Whisk until smooth and well blended. Soak the bread slices in the egg mixture until well absorbed and soft. Place the soaked slices on a baking sheet, wrap tightly, and store in refrigerator until you are ready to cook them.

To cook, heat two large nonstick skillets or a large griddle over medium heat. Melt 1 tablespoon of the butter; place several slices of bread on griddle and cook until golden brown, about 2 minutes on each side. Repeat with remaining slices and keep in a warm oven until ready to serve. Just before serving, toss the berries with the balsamic vinegar. Serve toasts on a long rectangular platter next to bowls of berries and Mascarpone cheese.

Serves 30.

SLICED MELONS AND BERRIES WITH MINTED HONEY-LIME DRESSING

An assortment of fresh fruit and berries is a welcome addition to any brunch buffet. Prepare the fruit and make the dressing the day before the shower and store in separate containers in the refrigerator.

$1/2$ CUP ORANGE CLOVER HONEY

$1/3$ CUP LIME JUICE, FRESHLY
    SQUEEZED

$1/2$ CUP CHOPPED FRESH MINT LEAVES

1 LARGE CANTALOUPE, CUT INTO
    CHUNKS OR MELON BALLS

1 LARGE HONEYDEW, CUT INTO
    CHUNKS OR MELON BALLS

1 PINT STRAWBERRIES, RINSED,
    HULLED, AND HALVED

1 PINT RASPBERRIES, RINSED

1 PINT BLUEBERRIES, RINSED

Place the honey, lime juice, and mint in a small bowl, whisking to combine. To serve, place the fruit in a large bowl and toss gently with the dressing.

Serves 30.

GLAZED LEMON BUNDT CAKE

A slightly sweet, lemony glaze offers a simple way to enhance the light flavors of this cake. We suggest
baking the cake in a bundt pan (two loaf pans would also work) the day before the shower and setting it aside
in a covered cake platter. Prepare the glaze the morning of the party.

For the cake:

2 CUPS CAKE FLOUR

$1^{1}/2$ CUPS SUPERFINE SUGAR

1 TEASPOON BAKING POWDER

1 TEASPOON SALT

6 EGGS, SEPARATED

$2/3$ CUP VEGETABLE OIL

$1/3$ CUP ORANGE JUICE

$1/3$ CUP LEMON JUICE

$1/4$ CUP CHOPPED LEMON ZEST

For the glaze:

$1/2$ CUP SUPERFINE SUGAR

$1/4$ CUP WATER

2 LEMONS, THINLY SLICED

Preheat oven to 350° F. Butter and flour a bundt pan and set aside. In a
large mixing bowl, sift together the flour and 1 cup of the sugar, the baking powder, and salt. In a separate bowl, whisk together the egg yolks, oil,
orange juice, lemon juice, and lemon zest. Beat the egg mixture into the
flour mixture until blended. In a third bowl, beat the egg whites with an
electric mixer until soft peaks form. Slowly add the remaining 1/2 cup
sugar and continue beating until egg whites are stiff. Fold one-third of
the egg whites into the batter. Fold in the remaining whites and stir until
just blended. Pour into the prepared pan and bake for 50 minutes, or
until a cake tester or toothpick comes out clean.

While the cake is cooling or the morning of the shower, make the glaze.
Combine the sugar and water in a small saucepan. Cook over medium
heat until boiling. Reduce heat, add the lemon slices, and cook until
the liquid has a slightly syrupy consistency and slices are soft (about
6 minutes). Remove the lemon slices with a slotted spoon and place on
the cake. Pour the glaze over the top of the cake and allow to drip down
the sides.

Serves 15 (you will need to make two cakes for 30 guests).

1 2 ③ 4 5

LUNCHEON FOR MOM

DECORATIONS

BUTTON PLACE CARDS

GINGHAM TABLECLOTH

MENU

CHILLED AVOCADO SOUP

HERB-CRUSTED BREADSTICKS

GRILLED SHRIMP SALAD WITH CITRUS-MANGO DRESSING

LIME SPRITZERS

ANGEL FOOD ICE DREAM CAKE WITH BERRY SAUCE

WATER WITH SLICED LEMONS

COFFEE / TEA

In the excitement and celebration of a shower, we sometimes focus all of our attention on preparing for the baby. As we shower the expected newborns with everything they might ever need for the first few years of their life, we sometimes lose sight of the needs of the mother-to-be. Inspired by the ancient Navajo practice of a "Blessingway," we created the Luncheon for Mom. Intended to be an intimate occasion, the Luncheon for Mom pays homage to the woman who has carried and nurtured her new baby for nearly nine months. Since the focus is on Mom rather than the baby, this is an ideal shower for a woman about to give birth a second or third time.

As with all of our showers, the decorating and menu ideas for the Luncheon for Mom sprang forth from a theme. In this case our theme was inspired by the colors of a vernal garden—spring green, pale pink, and yellow. Combining these three colors, we were able to create an ambience that was light, cheerful, and distinctly feminine.

Because the Luncheon for Mom is intended to be an intimate affair for no more than ten guests, you'll have lots of options for location. A lovely dining room, a covered porch, and a sunny pool deck can all provide an ideal setting. We opted for a garden. With its natural beauty and sweet fragrances, the garden setting was the perfect complement to our decorations and menu.

In keeping with the theme, we designed a light, healthful, and colorful menu. Carrying the colors of the garden into the food, we began the luncheon with a refreshing Lime Spritzer, and Chilled Avocado Soup accompanied by a basket of warm homemade Herb-Crusted Breadsticks. We followed with an entree of equal beauty and piquancy—a Grilled Shrimp Salad drizzled with Citrus Mango Dressing. To treat the mother-to-be with a sweet note on her special day, we served a fluffy white Angel Food Ice Dream Cake—the perfect dessert for a warm afternoon.

The focal point for this shower was a large, round table in the center of the garden. To the table, we added pink-and-white gingham linens and seating for ten. We selected gingham to pull a pattern into our decorating motif and to create a feminine ambience. In the center of the table, we placed a resplendent arrangement of ranunculus, garden roses, and viburnum in a pale green vase. The arrangement of deep and pale pinks interspersed with spring green reflected the natural beauty of the garden surroundings. We accented place cards with pink buttons and tiny yellow bows. As a reminder of the occasion, each rolled napkin was bound by a decorative pink pacifier that served as a napkin ring. Finally, to provide each guest with a little pampering of her own, we placed small cellophane bags filled with miniature beauty products and tied with pink gingham ribbons on everyone's seat.

What distinguishes the Luncheon for Mom from other baby showers is both the intimacy of the event and the attention devoted to the mother-to-be. To further pamper her at this special time, we like the idea of presenting gift certificates for facials, massages, manicures, or pedicures, or an overnight bag stuffed with all the items she will need to bring to the hospital. Another great idea is the gift of sessions with a personal trainer to help Mom return to her pre-pregnancy self. Finally, one of our favorite gifts is a box filled with a fluffy terry-cloth robe, comfy slippers, and an assortment of beauty products.

PUTTING IT TOGETHER

THREE OR FOUR DAYS AHEAD

Make Gingham Tablecloth
Make Button Place Cards
Tie napkins with pacifiers
Shop for food

TWO DAYS AHEAD

Receive and set up rentals
Pick up flowers, shop for last-minute ingredients
Make marinade and dressing for Grilled Shrimp Salad,
    keeping orange, mango, and green onion separate
Bake, assemble, and freeze Angel Food Ice Dream Cake

ONE DAY BEFORE

Set up the table and chairs for the luncheon and gifts
Make sure all table linens are ironed
Bake Herb-Crusted Breadsticks
Make Berry Sauce for Angel Food Cake
Arrange floral centerpiece

MORNING OF THE SHOWER

Make Chilled Avocado Soup
Set table with linens and dishware
Arrange place cards

A FEW HOURS BEFORE

Grill and assemble shrimp for salad
Slice lemons for water
Place flower petals on gift table
Juice limes for Lime Spritzers

JUST BEFORE THE SHOWER

Make coffee and tea
Fill glasses with water
Take ice-cream cake out of freezer
Make Lime Spritzers

BUTTON PLACE CARDS

The inclusion of place cards in your shower adds an extra touch of elegance. It also creates an opportunity to carry your theme even further. Here's a simple project that allows you to add a special note to everyday place cards.

1/4-INCH-WIDE YELLOW SATIN RIBBON OR PREMADE BOWS (AVAILABLE AT CRAFT STORES)

PINK BABY BUTTONS (VARIOUS SIZES)

WHITE TENT PLACE CARDS

GLUE GUN

PINK FELT-TIP PEN

Using the ribbon, make a small bow for each of your place cards. Place two buttons and a bow in the corner of each card to create a grouping you like. Using the glue gun, carefully adhere each button and bow. Allow the place cards to dry for 20 minutes before using the pen to inscribe the names of your guests.

GINGHAM TABLECLOTH

Pink gingham table linen will add just the right amount of color and pattern to your table and can be used again for any number of occasions. This recipe can be adjusted to fit any size table.

For a 90-inch-square tablecloth you will need:

5 1/4 YARDS PINK GINGHAM FABRIC
(46 INCHES WIDE)

Cut two 46-by-92-inch pieces. Match the right sides of the two large pieces of fabric and stitch along the long side, 1/4 inch from the edge. Press the seam open. You will have one square piece. Stitch a 1/4-inch hem around the rough edges and press with a warm iron to finish.

CHILLED AVOCADO SOUP

This refreshing and creamy soup is quickly made using ripe Haas avocados and canned vegetable stock. Prepare the soup the morning of the shower, and chill in a large pitcher until ready to serve.

---

7 RIPE HAAS AVOCADOS, PITTED,
    SKIN REMOVED

6 CUPS GOOD-QUALITY CANNED
    VEGETABLE STOCK

$1/4$ CUP CILANTRO LEAVES

3 TABLESPOONS LIME JUICE

$1/2$ TEASPOON GROUND WHITE PEPPER

$1/4$ TEASPOON CAYENNE PEPPER

10 SPRIGS CILANTRO

Chop five of the avocados into large chunks. Place the chopped avocados, vegetable stock, cilantro leaves, lime juice, and peppers in a food processor and process until well blended (you might have to do this in two batches). Adjust seasonings as needed. Place the soup in a large bowl or pitcher and refrigerate until well chilled. Slice the remaining two avocados lengthwise and reserve for garnish. To serve, ladle or pour into 10 bowls. Garnish with the avocado slices and a sprig of cilantro.

Serves 10.

HERB-CRUSTED BREADSTICKS

Working with frozen bread dough is an easy way to create interesting and fun shapes. These breadsticks can be seasoned with any combination of fresh or dried herbs. Bake them a day ahead of the shower and store in an airtight container.

FLOUR FOR WORK SURFACE

3 TABLESPOONS FRESH CHOPPED
    THYME LEAVES

3 TABLESPOONS CHOPPED FRESH
    ROSEMARY LEAVES

3 TABLESPOONS CHOPPED FRESH
    OREGANO LEAVES

ONE 3-POUND PACKAGE FROZEN
    BREAD DOUGH, THAWED

4 TABLESPOONS BUTTER, MELTED

Preheat oven to 375° F. On a lightly floured surface, knead all the herbs into the bread dough until evenly distributed. Roll dough into a log approximately 10 inches long. Slice the log into 10 pieces. Roll each slice into a thin rope shape and place on a parchment-lined baking sheet. Brush each breadstick with melted butter and bake for 15 minutes. Store in an airtight container until ready to serve.

Serves 10.

GRILLED SHRIMP SALAD

You can make this salad using grilled salmon, snapper, or even boneless chicken breast and substitute greens to complement the season. The marinade and dressing can be made two days in advance, leaving minimal last-minute preparation.

3/4 CUP OLIVE OIL

1/4 CUP LIME JUICE,
    FRESHLY SQUEEZED

1/4 CUP SHERRY VINEGAR

2 TABLESPOONS ORANGE JUICE
    CONCENTRATE

1 TEASPOON RED PEPPER FLAKES

1 TEASPOON SALT

1 TEASPOON PEPPER

1/4 CUP CHOPPED CHIVES

30 LARGE SHRIMP, PEELED
    AND DEVEINED

10 WOODEN SKEWERS, SOAKED
    IN WATER

3 POUNDS BABY LETTUCE GREENS

Combine the olive oil, lime juice, vinegar, orange juice concentrate, red pepper flakes, salt, pepper, and chives in a large bowl. Add the shrimp and marinate for a few hours. Thread shrimp on wooden skewers that have been soaked in water for 30 minutes. Heat an outdoor grill or stove-top grill pan to medium-high. Working quickly, grill shrimp in small batches until opaque and colorful, turning frequently. Serve immediately, or allow to cool to room temperature. To assemble salads, mound 2 cups of the baby greens in the center or each plate, top with three grilled shrimp, and finish with a generous spoonful of Citrus Mango Dressing (page 60).

Serves 10.

CITRUS-MANGO DRESSING

Prepare the dressing up to two days in advance, storing the mango, green onion, and orange in separate containers.

―――――――――――――――――――

2 TABLESPOONS SHERRY VINEGAR

2 TABLESPOONS ORANGE
JUICE CONCENTRATE

2 TABLESPOONS LIME JUICE,
FRESHLY SQUEEZED

2 TABLESPOONS LEMON JUICE,
FRESHLY SQUEEZED

2 TABLESPOONS DIJON MUSTARD

3/4 CUP OLIVE OIL

1 TEASPOON SALT

1/2 TEASPOON PEPPER

1 CUP MANGO, DICED

1 CUP ORANGE, SLICED BETWEEN
MEMBRANES, DICED

1/2 CUP GREEN ONION OR SCALLION,
THINLY SLICED

Combine the vinegar, orange juice concentrate, lime juice, lemon juice, and mustard in a small bowl to blend. Slowly whisk in the olive oil and season with the salt and pepper. Add the diced fruit and the onion, and stir to blend. Store at room temperature until ready to serve. Spoon over the baby greens and grilled shrimp.

Makes 2 cups.

LIME SPRITZER

The secret to this simple and refreshing drink is freshly squeezed lime juice. Multiply the basic
recipe by the number of drinks you need to serve, allowing for 2 or 3 per person.

JUICE OF 1 LIME

1 TABLESPOON SUPERFINE SUGAR

10 OUNCES CLUB SODA OR
    SODA WATER

ICE

LIME SLICE

In a tall glass, combine lime juice and superfine sugar. Add club soda
and stir well until ingredients are combined and sugar has dissolved. Fill
glass with ice and garnish rim of glass with lime slice.

Makes 1 drink.

ANGEL FOOD ICE DREAM CAKE WITH BERRY SAUCE

This simple recipe is embellished with a strawberry ice-cream filling and clouds of whipped cream, and garnished with berry sauce and sprigs of strawberry blossoms. Bake, fill, and decorate the cake up to two days in advance, and store in the freezer.

For the cake:

1 ANGEL FOOD CAKE, STORE-BOUGHT
    OR MADE FROM A BOX MIX

1 QUART PREMIUM STRAWBERRY
    ICE CREAM, SOFTENED

1 QUART CREAM, WHIPPED

For the sauce:

1 PINT FRESH STRAWBERRIES,
    QUARTERED

1/2 CUP SUGAR

1/4 CUP CHOPPED MINT

Slice the cake horizontally twice, making three layers. Separate the layers and place the bottom layer on a baking sheet lined with parchment. Spread half the softened ice cream over the bottom layer of cake and stack the second layer on top. Spread the second layer with the remaining softened ice cream and cover with the top layer. Freeze for 30 minutes. Meanwhile, using an electric mixer or wire whisk, whip the cream until stiff. Remove ice-cream cake from freezer and frost with the whipped cream, using the back of a spoon to make swirls. Return to freezer for up to 2 days.

To make the sauce, combine the strawberries, sugar, and mint in a bowl, and serve alongside the cake.

Serves 10.

1 2 3 ④ 5

DECORATING THE NURSERY

DECORATIONS AND GIFTS IDEAS

    PAINT CHIP INVITATIONS

    FOLDING NURSERY SHELVES

    CRIB OR BASSINET CANOPY

MENU

    PESTO CHICKEN WRAPS

    GRILLED VEGETABLE ANTIPASTO WITH GARLIC AIOLI

    MEDITERRANEAN POTATO SALAD

    LIME BARS

    BOTTLED BEVERAGES

The months before the arrival of a new baby are filled with excitement and anticipation. A favorite way for parents to prepare themselves during this time is by setting up a nursery in their home. Designing and decorating a nursery is a fun and memorable experience. So why not let family and friends join in the excitement? We created the Decorating the Nursery shower to be a truly useful party—a chance for six to eight family members and friends to gather to help prepare the new parents and to share in their once-in-a-lifetime experience. This party will need to be held in the home of the parents-to-be, so organize with them accordingly.

To reflect the decorating theme, we designed a handmade invitation assembled from paint chips. You can create your own by pulling paint chips in the colors of your nursery from the local hardware store. Simply cut the chips into rectangles and arrange them on plain white note cards in any pattern that suits you. A couple of hours and glue sticks later, you'll have constructed charming invitations ready for mailing. As you compose the invitation, be sure to remind your guests to wear work clothes or bring extra tools if necessary.

This shower is supposed to be both fun and productive, so it's important that you be organized. We recommend dividing the day's events into general categories such as hanging window treatments, assembling and moving furniture, cleaning crib linens, hanging pictures, and organizing the changing table. It is important that all the tasks are kept very orderly, since each person will have his or her own job. To that end, we set up two separate tables: one with color swatches, inspirational sketches, and each guest's assignments, and a second with all the tools required. Each guest simply visits the first table to see and read what he or she will be doing and then grabs the required tools from the second table. If repainting the entire room is part of your design, it's a good idea to have it done a week or two before the shower.

After all of their hard work, it's important to provide your guests with a hearty lunch. If you have access to a backyard or patio, we recommend setting up the meal on a picnic blanket—the outdoor setting provides a great way for your guests to relax and rejuvenate. To make the most of your time during the shower, we designed a menu that is easy to prepare a day in advance. We filled small blue buckets with Pesto Chicken Wraps and Mediterranean Potato Salad. To accompany the wraps we served a Grilled Vegetable Antipasto on a coordinating blue enamel platter. We capped off the meal with Lime Bars, a twist on popular lemon bars that can be left out for snacking on the rest of the day. You'll also want to provide plenty of beverages to quench your guests' thirst throughout the day. We recommend an ice chest or refrigerator full of bottled water and soft drinks.

Opening the gifts is a great way to finish off the day. We suggest asking each guest to bring an item to accessorize or stock the nursery. Baskets full of baby toiletries or boxes full of diapers make very practical gifts. Other ideas include crib linens wrapped in linen or muslin and tied with a beautiful trimming, yards of fabric to create the canopy over the bassinet, and a dryer rack painted and customized for use as shelving and storage. These gifts and many others add the final touch to a wonderful nursery and a successful afternoon.

PUTTING IT TOGETHER

FOUR WEEKS AHEAD

Make and send out Paint Chip Invitations

Make gift

TWO WEEKS AHEAD

Have nursery painted and ready to be decorated

THREE DAYS AHEAD

Have serving pieces, plates, and napkins ready for picnic

Have husband, friend, or neighbor arrange project tables

TWO DAYS AHEAD

Shop for groceries

Bake Lime Bars

Boil potatoes for Mediterranean Potato Salad

ONE DAY BEFORE

Put drinks in refrigerator

Assemble Pesto Chicken Wraps

Make Garlic Aioli

Slice vegetables for antipasto

MORNING OF THE SHOWER

Grill vegetables

Slice wraps

Bring potatoes to room temperature and dress salad

A FEW HOURS BEFORE

Arrange vegetable antipasto on platter

Place wraps in bucket

Place potato salad in bucket

Slice Lime Bars and dust with powdered sugar

JUST BEFORE THE SHOWER

Pour water into pitcher or decanter with ice

Set drinks on table

RENOIR BLUE

BLUE WALTZ

P 2018-3

M 2018-1

BLUE WALTZ

DAINTY BLUE

P 2018-5

A2-4

BRIGHT WHITE

PAINT CHIP INVITATIONS

Mystify your guests with your own masterpiece of modern design. Who would have thought a collage of paint chips could ever look so good? Don't worry if you're not Piet Mondrian; anyone can arrange colored rectangles (he just did it first).

X-ACTO KNIFE

VARIOUS PAINT CHIPS FROM
    HARDWARE STORE

6¹/₄-BY-4¹/₂-INCH WHITE NOTE CARDS

GLUE STICK

Using the knife, carefully cut paint chips from paint cards. Design a pattern with the paint chips on a note card. Adhere each chip with the glue stick. Remember to glue one at a time in order to maintain your pattern. Repeat with the remaining chips and cards. Allow to dry overnight before writing the party information inside.

FOLDING NURSERY SHELVES

Turn a plain wooden drying rack into an attractive and functional piece of furniture. This isn't a difficult project, but if carpentry isn't your strong suit you may want to get a friend to help out. We've designed this recipe for a rack that is 2 feet wide, but you can adjust the measurements to fit a different size rack.

FOUR $1/4$-INCH PINE WOOD STRIPS $1^1/2$-BY-21 INCHES FOR SHELF FACES (LENGTH MAY VARY)

2 PIECES $1/4$-INCH PINE OR BIRCH PLYWOOD 15-BY-21 INCHES FOR SHELVES (MEASUREMENT FOR YOUR RACK MAY VARY)

WOOD GLUE

CORDLESS DRILL

SCREWDRIVER

EIGHT $1/2$-INCH WOOD SCREWS

WOOD PUTTY

PUTTY KNIFE

FINE-GRADE SANDPAPER

PAINTBRUSH

PRIMER

WHITE HIGH-GLOSS ENAMEL PAINT

WOODEN ACCORDION-STYLE CLOTHES-DRYING RACK

To make a shelf, place one strip of pine wood at a 90 degree angle, flush with the top of the plywood. Drill a small pilot hole on each side of the shelf and into the plywood. Repeat on the other side of the shelf. Remove the pine strip and apply wood glue along the long edge. Reposition the strip and countersink two screws in the pilot holes. Wipe off excess glue. Attach another pine strip to the opposite long side of the plywood in the same manner. Repeat to make the second shelf.

Work the wood putty into the depressions of the screws and smooth with a putty knife to create a flat, even surface. When dry, lightly sand the puttied areas and any rough surfaces in the wood until smooth.

Following the manufacturer's directions, prime the entire rack and shelves and allow it to dry completely.

Sand any rough areas and remove dust before applying the first coat of white paint. Apply the paint to rack and shelves and allow it to dry completely. Sand any imperfections or rough spots in the paint and remove dust. Apply a second coat of paint and allow to dry for at least 24 hours.

Position the shelves onto the drying rack and stock as desired. To prevent the nursery shelves from falling over, attach an L-shaped bracket to the back of the rack and secure to the wall, preferably at the wall studs.

CRIB OR BASSINET CANOPY

Embellish the baby's sleeping area with this simple canopy. We used a blue striped seersucker fabric for this project, but sheers like chiffon, tulle, and cotton theatrical scrim work equally well. You many want to double up on fabric and/or increase the width to give the canopy a fuller look.

SEWING MACHINE

3 YARDS 60-INCH-WIDE FABRIC
(THIS MAY NEED TO BE ADJUSTED
ACCORDING TO YOUR ROOM
DIMENSIONS)

DECORATIVE HOOK

Measure the height of the ceiling in the nursery, and add 14 inches to allow fabric to be gathered at the top and draped gracefully around the floor. This will be the length of the canopy. Using a sewing machine, hem the edges around the entire piece of fabric. Gather the fabric at the top end (where it will hang from ceiling) and make a knot as close to the edge as possible. Screw the decorative hook into the ceiling over the center point of where you would like the canopy to drape. Find space in the knot and slide it over the hook to secure. Fluff fabric around the crib or bassinet to finish.

PESTO CHICKEN WRAPS

Ingredients can be purchased from a good-quality market or gourmet shop a couple of days before the party.
Assemble the wraps the day before to free up time the day of the shower.

---

8 OUNCES GOAT CHEESE

8 OUNCES CREAM CHEESE

1 PACKAGE 12-INCH WRAPS

16 OUNCES PACKAGED PESTO

ONE 4-POUND ROASTED ROTISSERIE
    CHICKEN, PULLED INTO 1$^1/_2$- TO
    2-INCH SHREDS

ONE 16-OUNCE JAR SUN-DRIED
    TOMATOES IN OIL, DRAINED AND
    CUT INTO THIN STRIPS

In a food processor, blend the goat cheese and cream cheese until smooth and spreadable. Spread four wraps with the cheese mixture followed by a thin layer of pesto, pulled chicken, and a few sun-dried tomatoes. Roll each wrap as tightly as possible into a large cylinder. Wrap with plastic wrap to keep from drying out, and refrigerate at least two hours or overnight. Remove plastic wrap and roll with parchment paper, twisting each end to secure. Cut in half on a diagonal and serve.

Serves 8.

GRILLED VEGETABLE ANTIPASTO WITH GARLIC AIOLI

Practically any firm vegetable in season can be substituted for the vegetables used in this recipe.
We chose the vegetables below for their variety of colors and shapes. Roasted garlic tastes especially wonderful
when blended into a creamy aioli to serve with the veggies.

For the garlic aioli:

1 HEAD GARLIC, TOP CUT
    TO EXPOSE CLOVES

1 TABLESPOON OLIVE OIL

1 CUP MAYONNAISE

2 TABLESPOONS CHOPPED FRESH BASIL

SALT AND PEPPER TO TASTE

For the grilled vegetables:

1 TABLESPOON DIJON MUSTARD

1/2 TEASPOON EACH SALT AND PEPPER

1 TEASPOON FRESH THYME

1 TEASPOON CHOPPED FRESH ROSEMARY

1/4 CUP RED WINE VINEGAR

3/4 CUP OLIVE OIL

1 EGGPLANT

2 ZUCCHINIS

2 RED OR YELLOW PEPPERS

2 RED ONIONS

1 POUND ASPARAGUS

To make the aioli, heat oven to 350° F. Place the garlic head on a square of aluminum foil and drizzle with the olive oil. Fold foil up around garlic to form a sealed packet. Roast in oven for about 45 minutes, until garlic is soft, fragrant, and slightly browned. Remove from oven and cool. Peel back papery skin and separate to remove soft cloves. In a food processor, blend the mayonnaise, roasted garlic, and basil until smooth and creamy. Season with salt and pepper.

Makes 1 cup.

To make the grilled vegetables, combine the first six ingredients in a small bowl, whisking to blend. Slice the eggplant crosswise into 1/2-inch slices. Slice the zucchinis lengthwise into 1/4-inch slices. Core the peppers and cut lengthwise into eighths. Cut the onions into eighths. Cut the asparagus into 5- to 6-inch lengths. Lay the cut vegetables out on a large baking sheet and brush generously with the marinade. Heat an outdoor grill or stovetop grill pan to medium-high heat. Grill the vegetables for 3 to 5 minutes on each side, brushing with marinade until softened and lined with grill marks. Vegetables can be grilled the morning of the shower and kept refrigerated. Bring to room temperature before serving.

Serves 8.

MEDITERRANEAN POTATO SALAD

There are many varieties of unusual potatoes available at the farmers' market. We chose three
varieties, each with unique characteristics. Potatoes keep well even after they've been cooked, so this recipe
can be made up to two days before the shower.

2 POUNDS BABY RED POTATOES

1 POUND BABY WHITE POTATOES

2 POUNDS BABY PURPLE POTATOES

2 TABLESPOONS CHOPPED FRESH
    ROSEMARY

2 TABLESPOONS CHOPPED PARSLEY

1/2 CUP SHERRY VINEGAR

3 TABLESPOONS LEMON JUICE,
    FRESHLY SQUEEZED

1/2 CUP OLIVE OIL

8 OUNCES CRUMBLED FETA CHEESE

8 OUNCES KALAMATA OLIVES,
    PITTED AND CHOPPED

SALT AND PEPPER TO TASTE

Bring a large pot of salted water to a boil. Cut the potatoes in half (do not
peel) and boil for about 12 minutes, until tender. Remove from heat and
drain. While still warm, place in a large bowl and toss with the remaining
ingredients. If preparing in advance, store in an airtight container in the
refrigerator. Bring to room temperature and toss with additional dressing
before serving.

Serves 8.

LIME BARS

Fresh lime juice is the key to this pleasantly tart treat. Bake up to two days in advance and slice into bars.
Sprinkle with powdered sugar and garnish with a mini lime wedge before serving.

---

1 1/2 CUPS PLUS 1 TABLESPOON
ALL-PURPOSE FLOUR

1/2 CUP POWDERED SUGAR,
PLUS EXTRA FOR DUSTING

3/4 CUP BUTTER, CUT INTO PIECES,
ROOM TEMPERATURE

4 EGGS

1 1/2 CUPS GRANULATED SUGAR

1/2 CUP FRESH LIME JUICE

1 TABLESPOON GRATED LIME PEEL

3 LIME SLICES, QUARTERED

Preheat oven to 350° F. Combine the 1 1/2 cups flour and 1/2 cup powdered sugar in a large bowl. Add the butter and cut in until the mixture resembles coarse meal. Press mixture into the bottom of 7-by-12-by-2-inch baking dish. Bake until golden brown, about 20 minutes. Remove from oven and maintain oven temperature. Beat the eggs, 1 1/2 cups granulated sugar, lime juice, lime peel, and remaining 1 tablespoon flour in a bowl to blend. Pour into the crust. Bake until the mixture is set, about 20 minutes. Allow to cool. Cut into 12 bars, sift powdered sugar over the top, and garnish with the lime slices.

Makes 12 bars.

1 2 3 4 ⑤

HEIRLOOMS AND MEMORIES

DECORATIONS, FAVORS, AND GIFT IDEAS

SCRAPBOOK

HEIRLOOM QUILT

CITRUS MARZIPAN FAVORS

TRIMMED BANNER, RUNNER, AND NAPKINS

CITRUS CLUSTERS

MENU

SWEET POTATO CHIPS

GRILLED CHICKEN CAESAR SANDWICHES

CITRUS SLAW

LEMON POPPY SEED CUPCAKES WITH BUTTER FROSTING
AND CANDIED LEMON STRIPS

ASSORTMENT OF BOTTLED DRINKS

The Heirlooms and Memories shower is probably the most traditional shower in this book. It's also the easiest to prepare and host. Thrown in the home of a friend or loved one, what makes this shower unique is the theme. Each guest brings an heirloom, a special item that has been passed from generation to generation, or a handmade gift. The perfect shower for the mother who already has everything she'll need or a mother giving birth a second time, this shower provides gifts and memories that will be cherished for a lifetime.

As a complement to the theme, we chose to decorate with a citrus motif. The vibrant oranges and yellows create a warm and cheery ambience perfectly befitting the occasion. We also felt that the luminous colors of the citrus palette were symbolic of the radiance, warmth, and joy a new baby brings to every family. Building on the motif even further, we pulled citrus accents and flavors into the luncheon and desserts.

This easy-to-prepare menu can be made a day ahead of time. At the center of the luncheon is a Grilled Chicken Caesar Sandwich, which strikes the perfect balance between the pleasing flavors of garlic and lemon. Prepared in advance, this sandwich becomes even more delicious as all of the flavors marinate and meld overnight. To help keep all of their tasty ingredients between the bread and out of the guests' laps, the sandwiches are wrapped in parchment paper, tied with twine, and cut into individual servings. Accenting the Caesar sandwich, we offer crispy Sweet Potato Chips, a crunchy twist on tradition, and a tangy Citrus Slaw infused with the intricate flavors of oranges, fennel, endive, raisins, and pecans and tossed in a savory dressing. Of course, no luncheon would be complete without a sweet finish. Carrying the citrus theme into the dessert, Lemon Poppy Seed Cupcakes are topped with swirls of white butter frosting and Candied

Lemon Strips. For beverages, we supplied bottled water and a favorite childhood indulgence—old-fashioned orange soda.

The coordinating table linens, napkins, and banner were made from yellow cotton fabric trimmed with orange grosgrain ribbon. After hanging the banner behind the buffet table, we accented its corners with clusters of citrus fruits—oranges, lemons, and kumquats bunched and wired together. In the center of the table we placed a footed white compote brimming with citrus fruits and dotted with delicate orange blossoms. For the favor, we wrapped orange- and lemon-shaped marzipan fruits in melon-colored netting tied with green floral wire.

Of course, the most memorable aspect of this shower is the gifts. Heirlooms such as an antique silver rattle, an antique baby cup, a vintage christening gown, a special piece of jewelry, or a favorite childhood toy are heartfelt gifts that will be treasured for years and can eventually be passed along to the next generation. For those without an heirloom to give, a keepsake or large jewelry box in which to store the heirlooms makes a great gift. We've also created unique handmade items for those with the time to make their gifts. A fabric-covered scrapbook filled with images and news clippings from the year the baby is born creates a time capsule of memories that the mother and child will cherish. A quilt sewn from swatches of the mother's maternity clothes, old family blankets, or a grandparent's wardrobe creates a one-of-a-kind blanket.

PUTTING IT TOGETHER

FOUR DAYS AHEAD
- Make and wrap gift
- Sew Trimmed Banner, Runner, and Napkins
- Make Citrus Marzipan Favors

THREE DAYS AHEAD
- Shop for food
- Purchase paper containers for Citrus Slaw
- Purchase bottled beverages
- Purchase citrus fruits for centerpiece and Citrus Clusters
- Have all serving pieces ready

TWO DAYS AHEAD
- Make Citrus Slaw dressing and toast pecans
- Make Candied Lemon Strips for Lemon Poppy Seed cupcakes
- Make Caesar dressing
- Make Citrus Clusters

ONE DAY BEFORE
- Grill, assemble, and wrap Chicken Caesar Sandwiches
- Prep ingredients for Citrus Slaw; keep separate
- Make Lemon Poppy Seed Cupcakes
- Set buffet table
- Hang banner and Citrus Clusters

MORNING OF THE SHOWER
- Arrange favors on table
- Arrange centerpiece
- Slice Chicken Caesar Sandwiches and place on cutting board
- Assemble Citrus Slaw in containers
- Frost cupcakes and garnish with Candied Lemon Strips
- Make Sweet Potato Chips

JUST BEFORE THE SHOWER
- Set bottled drinks on tables with straws
- Place food on table

SCRAPBOOK

This is our most difficult project, but it's worth the effort. This scrapbook is more than a treasured keepsake; it's a time capsule that friends and family can fill with important mementos from the year in which the child is born.

METAL RULER

X-ACTO KNIFE

2 SHEETS 36-BY-24-INCH DOUBLE-PLY
CHIPBOARD

$1^1/_2$ YARDS FABRIC, IRONED

FABRIC GLUE

$^1/_8$-INCH HOLE PUNCH

1 PACK 12-BY-12-INCH ARCHIVAL
SCRAPBOOK PAPER

$^1/_2$ YARD $^1/_8$-INCH-WIDE SILK RIBBON,
CUT INTO THREE 6-INCH PIECES

Using the ruler and the X-acto knife, measure and cut two 12 $^1/_4$-by-12 $^1/_4$-inch squares and two 11-by-11-inch squares of chipboard. Be patient; you will have to run the knife down each side several times before it cuts through the chipboard. Cut the fabric into two 14-by-14-inch squares (to cover the larger chipboard squares) and two 13-by-13-inch squares (to cover the smaller chipboard squares).

Lay a 14-by-14-inch fabric square face down and apply fabric glue along the inside edge of fabric. Place a 12 $^1/_4$-by-12 $^1/_4$-inch chipboard square in the center of the fabric square. Fold over and glue the fabric to the chipboard. Pull tightly and fold the corners carefully, creating a smooth surface. Repeat the above step for the remaining squares. Let dry for 30 minutes.

To create the front cover, lay a 12 $^1/_4$-by-12 $^1/_4$-inch square fabric side down and glue the 11-by-11-inch square on top of it, fabric side up. Repeat the above step to create the back cover. Let dry for 30 minutes.

Using a ruler, measure three holes evenly along the front cover and mark lightly with a pencil. Using the hole punch, push through marks to create three holes (this step requires some strength). Repeat procedure on the back cover. Line up the scrapbook paper with the holes on the covers. Punch holes through the scrapbook pages. Insert a ribbon through each hole, pull taut, and tie a bow. Now you are ready to fill the pages!

HEIRLOOM QUILT

Many of us fondly recall a childhood quilt or blanket. Here's an opportunity for you to create a prized memory for baby. Don't panic if you can't sew; just provide supplies and the directions below to a seamstress, who will be able to knock out this project in very little time and at little expense. The finished quilt will measure approximately 32-by-32 inches.

FABRIC SCRAPS AND SWATCHES
(ENOUGH TO CREATE SIXTY-FOUR
4-INCH SQUARES)

SEWING MACHINE

1 YARD QUILT LINING

1 YARD TERRY-CLOTH FABRIC

4 YARDS TRIMMING

From the fabric swatches, cut out sixty-four 4-inch squares of fabric. Lay out the squares in eight rows of eight to create a pattern you like. Use the sewing machine to stitch the squares together with a 1/4 -inch seam allowance. It's easiest if you stitch your 8 square rows first, then stitch the 8 finished rows together. Pressing between stitching will give you clean, even results.

Lay the quilt lining flat and lay the finished quilt face on top of it. Trim the quilt lining to fit the quilt face. Set lining and quilt face aside.

Cut a 33-inch square of terry-cloth fabric and lay it flat on your work surface. Center the quilt lining on top, leaving an even border of terry-cloth fabric around the lining. Lay the quilt face right side up on top of the lining, matching edges. At the corners of the quilt face, turn down each of the four edges of the terry cloth, pinning through all thicknesses.

Fold the extra border of terry cloth over the edge of the quilt face and pin the edges down. Stitch around the quilt edge, sewing through all thicknesses. Position the trimming over the edge of the terry cloth, pinning it down. Stitch around the quilt, securing trimming to the quilt.

CITRUS MARZIPAN FAVORS

These simple favors are both beautiful and delicious. If you're short on time, you might
want to skip this step by asking a local bakery to make the marzipan fruits for you.

THREE 8.8 OZ. BOXES OF MARZIPAN
   (FOUND AT MOST WELL-STOCKED
   SUPERMARKETS)

1 BOTTLE YELLOW FOOD COLORING

1 BOTTLE RED FOOD COLORING

TINY LEAVES AND FLOWERS (OPTIONAL)

60 WHOLE CLOVES

1/2 YARD ORANGE OR MELON TULLE

1 ROLL GREEN CLOTH-COVERED
   FLORAL WIRE

Gently form the marzipan dough into two equal balls. Press your thumb into the middle of the first ball to form an indentation in the center. Place about seven or eight drops of yellow and two or three drops of red food coloring into the indentation. Using your hands, work the coloring into the dough until evenly distributed throughout. Continue adding more yellow and/or red to achieve the shade of orange you want. Repeat with the other ball of dough, using more yellow and less red to achieve the shade of yellow you want.

Form the orange dough into miniature oranges, creating the shape with your hands. They should be about 3/4 inch in diameter. Do the same with the yellow dough, forming it into miniature lemon shapes. Pinch each end slightly to give it an elongated shape. To finish the oranges, place a tiny leaf and flower near the top and press a clove "stem" to secure the end.

To make the pouches, cut the tulle into 4-inch squares, place three or four citrus marzipans in the center, and gather the fabric around them. Secure with a 5-inch piece of the cloth-covered wire. Curl ends to form a loose spiral.

Yields approximately 20 favors (3 fruits per favor).

TRIMMED BANNER, RUNNER, AND NAPKINS

These easy and beautiful linens combine two pale citrus colors. We chose inexpensive cotton fabric and cotton grosgrain ribbon.

For the banner, you will need:

3 YARDS (30 INCHES WIDE)
    PALE YELLOW FABRIC

8 1/2 YARDS (1 INCH WIDE) PALE
    ORANGE GROSGRAIN RIBBON

For the runner, you will need:

1 1/4 YARDS (46 INCHES WIDE)
    PALE YELLOW FABRIC

5 1/2 YARDS (1 INCH WIDE) PALE
    ORANGE GROSGRAIN RIBBON

*For 20 (14-by-14-inch) napkins,
you will need:*

3 YARDS (46 INCHES WIDE)
    PALE YELLOW FABRIC

34 YARDS (3/8 INCH WIDE) PALE
    ORANGE GROSGRAIN RIBBON
    (OPTIONAL)

Measure and cut fabric to sizes described. For all linens, fold and press edges under to create a 1/4-inch hem. Place ribbon on top of hem and stitch around the edges to secure.

For the banner, leave crisscrossing pieces of ribbon (6 to 8 inches long) at each of the two top corners. These will allow the banner to be tied to the wall or ceiling.

CITRUS CLUSTERS

Clusters of citrus fruits tied at either end of your banner are beautiful embellishments.
Use firm, thick-skinned fruits for the best results.

For two citrus clusters, you will need:

WOODEN SKEWER

10 TO 12 ORANGES WITH FIRM SKINS

10 TO 12 LEMONS WITH FIRM SKINS

20 TO 24 KUMQUATS

18-GAUGE FLORAL WIRE (18 INCHES
  EACH PIECE)

2 CUP HOOKS

Using the skewer, pierce each piece of citrus through its top and thread the wire through the hole. Pull wire through so that there is an equal length of wire on each side of the fruit, then gather and twist the wire at the top of the fruit. Continue wiring each piece of fruit. Make one cluster by gathering half the wired fruits near the top of the wire and twisting all the wires together. Repeat to make the second cluster.

Screw the cup hooks into the wall or ceiling, where the banner will be secured. First tie the banner to the hooks, then attach the citrus clusters by wrapping the wires carefully around each hook to secure.

SWEET POTATO CHIPS

Here is a nice variation on an old favorite. The sweet potatoes have high sugar content, so they must be cooked for a longer time at a lower temperature. Use a Japanese slicer or a French mandoline to slice the sweet potatoes paper thin. You can use a deep pan with high sides for frying, but a tabletop consumer fryer works best.

1 QUART CORN OIL OR PEANUT
OIL FOR FRYING

2 MEDIUM TO LARGE SWEET
POTATOES, PEELED

SALT TO TASTE

Heat oil in a heavy, high-sided pot, or a fryer with a thermostat. Use a cooking thermometer and adjust heat to keep the temperature of oil at 325° F. Slice the sweet potatoes paper thin with either a vegetable slicer or a sharp knife. When oil has come to temperature, fry 8 to 10 chips at a time, for approximately 5 to 6 minutes. Chips should be a deep golden brown color, with slightly brown edges. Drain on paper towels and sprinkle with salt to taste. Let the oil come back to 325° before adding another batch. Store in an airtight container.

Makes approximately 100 chips.

GRILLED CHICKEN CAESAR SANDWICHES

Plan to make this recipe the day before the shower, which will allow the flavors to intensify. The morning of the party, simply slice the sandwiches into individual portions and serve.

8 CHICKEN BREASTS, BONELESS
   AND SKINLESS

3/4 CUP PLUS 4 TABLESPOONS
   OLIVE OIL

8 CLOVES GARLIC, MINCED

2 TABLESPOONS PLUS 1 TEASPOON
   CRACKED PEPPER

3 LEMONS, SLICED AND BRUSHED
   LIGHTLY WITH OLIVE OIL

1 TABLESPOON DIJON MUSTARD

1/3 CUP LEMON JUICE

1 CLOVE GARLIC, PEELED

3 ANCHOVIES, CHOPPED, OR
   1 TABLESPOON ANCHOVY PASTE

2 LONG LOAVES CRUSTY RUSTIC BREAD

2 HEADS ROMAINE LETTUCE, WASHED,
   LEAVES SEPARATED

1/4 POUND PARMESAN CHEESE, SHAVED

Rub the chicken breasts with the 4 tablespoons olive oil. Combine the minced garlic and the 2 tablespoons pepper and rub into the chicken. Grill the chicken over medium heat on an outdoor grill or in a grill pan on a stovetop for 4 to 6 minutes on each side, or until done. Remove the chicken, maintain heat, and grill the lemon slices until lightly charred on each side. Place one or two lemon slices on each chicken breast.

Combine the mustard, lemon juice, garlic cloves, anchovies, and remaining 1 teaspoon pepper in a food processor and pulse until well blended. With the processor running, slowly pour the remaining 3/4 cup olive oil until emulsified with the other ingredients.

Slice the bread loaves in half lengthwise and tear out the center of each piece, leaving approximately 1 inch of bread on crusts. Brush generously with dressing. Toss the romaine leaves with the remaining dressing.

To assemble the sandwiches, place the chicken breasts end to end lengthwise along the bottom halves of the loaves. Layer with the dressed lettuce leaves and top with the Parmesan shavings. Place tops of bread on sandwiches, wrap tightly with parchment paper, and tie with string or twine about every 4 inches. Refrigerate overnight. Slice between string ties before serving.

Serves 10.

CITRUS SLAW

The ingredients can be prepped up to two days before the party, keeping the dressing, orange sections, and slaw in three separate containers. Whisk the dressing vigorously before tossing the slaw.

1 TEASPOON DIJON MUSTARD

1 TABLESPOON SOY SAUCE

1/4 CUP ORANGE JUICE CONCENTRATE

1/4 CUP SEASONED RICE VINEGAR

1/2 CUP VEGETABLE OIL

5 HEADS ENDIVE, SLICED CROSSWISE INTO 3/4-INCH PIECES

1 LARGE FENNEL BULB, SLICED CROSSWISE INTO 1/4-INCH PIECES

3 LARGE ORANGES, RIND AND PITHS REMOVED, SLICED BETWEEN MEMBRANES IN SECTIONS

1/2 CUP GOLDEN RAISINS

1/2 CUP PECAN PIECES, LIGHTLY TOASTED

Combine the mustard, soy sauce, juice concentrate, and vinegar in a small bowl. Add the vegetable oil in a slow, steady stream, while whisking continuously until all the ingredients are well blended.

Place the endive, fennel, orange sections, raisins, and pecans in a large bowl and toss with dressing.

Serves 10.

LEMON POPPY SEED CUPCAKES WITH BUTTER FROSTING AND CANDIED LEMON STRIPS

There is nothing better than this combination of light lemony cake, tiny crunchy poppy seeds, and creamy butter frosting. The Candied Lemon Strips can be made up to two days ahead. The cupcakes and frosting can be prepared and baked the day before.

For the lemon strips:

3 LEMONS, SCRUBBED AND DRIED

1 EGG WHITE, BEATEN

1/2 CUP SUPERFINE SUGAR

For the cake:

1 BOX LEMON CAKE MIX

ONE 3 1/2-OZ BOX LEMON PUDDING MIX

1/4 CUP VEGETABLE OIL

3 EGGS, BEATEN

1/4 CUP WATER

1/4 CUP FRESH LEMON JUICE

2 TABLESPOONS CHOPPED LEMON ZEST

3 TABLESPOONS POPPY SEEDS

For the frosting:

1/2 CUP UNSALTED BUTTER,
    ROOM TEMPERATURE

3 CUPS POWDERED SUGAR, SIFTED

4 TABLESPOONS HEAVY CREAM

1 TEASPOON VANILLA EXTRACT

Up to two days and at least one day before the shower, make the lemon strips. Using a paring knife, cut wide slices of rind from the lemon. Trim the white pith from the underside of the slices. Cut the lemon rinds into 24 thin strips. Curl each strip around your finger, brush with egg white, and dust liberally with sugar. Set the sugared strips on a clean baking sheet and place in a warm, dry spot overnight. Or place the sheet in a 200° F oven for 3 or 4 hours, until dry.

To make the cake, first preheat oven to 350° F. Line muffin tins with paper baking cups. In a large bowl, combine the cake mix and pudding mix, and stir to blend. Add the oil, eggs, water, and lemon juice, stirring after each addition. Add the lemon zest and poppy seeds and stir until just blended. Pour into the prepared muffin tins. Bake for 15 to 18 minutes, or until a cake tester or toothpick comes out clean. Allow to cool before frosting.

While the cakes are cooling or the morning of the shower, make the frosting. Cream the butter. Add the remaining ingredients, and continue creaming until the mixture is well blended and fluffy. Frost the cupcakes and decorate with the Candied Lemon Strips.

Serves 24.

RESOURCES

CRAFT SUPPLIES AND ART PAPERS

Aahs
3223 Wilshire Boulevard
Santa Monica, CA 90403
310-829-1807
wrapping paper, boxes, tissue

Kate's Paperie
561 Broadway
New York, NY 10012
212-941-9816
papers, craft supplies, pens,
invitations, wrapping

Michael's Arts & Crafts
972-409-7660 (customer relations)
craft supplies

Moskatel's
733 South San Julian Street
Los Angeles, CA 90014
213-689-4830
craft supplies

Paper Access
1-800-PAPER-01
papers, stationery, envelopes, tissue;
catalog available

Pearl Art Supply
800-451-7327
art and craft supplies

Soolip Paperie
8646 Melrose Avenue
West Hollywood, CA 90069
310-360-0545
stationery, papers, pens, envelopes, cards;
printing service available

Standard Brands Party
3020 Wilshire Boulevard
Santa Monica, CA 90403
310-453-1094
party supplies, boxes, wrapping

Stats Floral Supply
120 South Raymond Avenue
Pasadena, CA 91105
626-795-9308
party, craft, and themed supplies, silk flowers

FABRICS, NOTIONS, RIBBONS

B & J Fabrics
263 West 40th Street
New York, NY 10018
212-354-8150
fabrics

Bell'occhio
8 Brady Street
San Francisco, CA 94103
415-864-4048
new and vintage ribbons

Britex Fabrics
146 Geary Street
San Francisco, CA 94108
415-392-2910
fabrics

F & S Fabrics
10629 West Pico Boulevard
Los Angeles, CA 90064
310-470-3398
fabrics, ribbons, trimmings, notions

Hyman Hendler & Sons
67 West 38th Street
New York, NY 10018
212-840-8393
or
729 East Temple Street
Los Angeles, CA 90012
ribbons, trimmings, fabric

Lincoln Fabrics
1600 Lincoln Boulevard
Venice, CA 90291
310-396-5724
fabrics, ribbons, trimmings, some vintage

M & J Trimming
1008 Sixth Avenue
New York, NY 10018
212-391-9072
trimming, buttons

Rosen & Chadick
246 West 40th Street
New York, NY 10018
212-869-0142
fabrics

Silk Trading Company
351 South La Brea Avenue
Los Angeles, CA 90036
323-954-9280
silk fabrics

Tinsel Trading
47 West 38th Street
New York, NY 10018
212-730-1030
new and vintage trimmings

HOUSEWARES AND FURNITURE

ABC Carpet & Home
888 Broadway
New York, NY 10003
212-473-3000
home accessories, furniture, baby furniture,
linens, bath accessories, baby products

Anthropologie
800-309-2500
www.anthropologie.com
tabletop, home accessories, linens, baby products

Banana Republic Home
888-906-2800
tabletop, linens

Bellini
888-772-2291
baby furniture, clothes, and accessories

Bountiful
1335 Abbot Kinney Boulevard
Venice, CA 90291
310-450-3620
antique tableware, vases, linens

Calvin Klein Home
800-294-7978
tabletop, linens

Crate & Barrel
800-451-8217
tabletop, kitchenware

Fillamento
2185 Fillmore
San Francisco, CA 94115
415-931-2224
tabletop, home accessories, linens,
bath accessories

Garnet Hill
800-622-6216
catalog only
baby linens and furniture

IKEA
800-434-4532
www.ikea.com
tabletop, linens, kitchen, furniture,
baby furniture

Maison Midi
150 South La Brea
Los Angeles, CA 90036
323-935-3154
tabletop, linens

Pom Pom
326 North La Brea
Los Angeles, CA 90036
323-934-2051
housewares, antiques and vintage
linens and fabrics

Pottery Barn
800-588-6250
tabletop, linens, home accessories,
baby furniture

Restoration Hardware
800-762-1005
tabletop, home accessories

Room with a View
1600 Montana Avenue
Santa Monica, CA 90403
310-998-5858
tabletop, linens, baby furniture, baby gifts

ShanRose Designs
18740 Oxnard Street, #316
Tarzana, CA 91356
818-996-4747
home accessories

Shelter
7920 Beverly Boulevard
Los Angeles, CA 90048
323-937-3222
tabletop, home accessories

Sue Fisher King
3067 Sacramento Street
San Francisco, CA 94115
415-922-7276
tabletop, linens

Target
800-800-8800
stores nationwide
housewares and party supplies

Waterworks
800-998-2284
stores nationwide
bath accessories, linens, toiletries

Wolfman Gold & Good Co.
117 Mercer Street
New York, NY 10012
212-431-1888
tabletop

Zona
97 Greene Street
New York, NY 10012
212-925-6750
home accessories, tabletop

KITCHENWARE AND BAKING SUPPLIES

Broadway Panhandler
477 Broome Street
New York, NY 10013
212-966-3434
gourmet kitchenware and baking supplies

Dean & Deluca
800-999-0306
*gourmet kitchenware, tabletop and
baking supplies*

NY Cake & Baking
56 West 22nd Street
New York, NY 10010
212-675-2253

Sur La Table
800-243-0852
call for store locations

Williams-Sonoma
800-541-2233
call for store locations

SKIN AND HAIR CARE

Kiehl's
109 Third Avenue
New York, NY 10003
212-677-3171 or 1-800-KIE-HLS1
Products for adults and babies

FLOWERS/GARDENING

B & J Florists Supply
103 West 28th Street
New York, NY 10001
212-564-6086
floral and craft supplies

Bill's Flower Market
816 Sixth Avenue
New York, NY 10001
212-889-8154
floral and craft supplies

Hortus
284 East Orange Grove Boulevard
Pasadena, CA 91104
626-792-8255
gardening gifts, plants, flowers

Mellano & Company
766 Wall Street
Los Angeles, CA 90014
213-622-0796
public sales hours: Mon., Wed., Fri.
8:00 AM—12:00 PM; Tues., Thurs.,
Sat. 6:00 PM—12:00 PM
fresh cut flowers and foliage

LINENS AND BEDDING

Koo Koo
512 Beatty Street
Vancouver, BC V6B 6GB
Canada
604-844-7445
towels, baby linens

Portico Home
72 Spring Street
New York, NY 10012
212-941-7800
linens, bath accessories

Tocca Casa
2123 Montana Avenue
Santa Monica, CA 90403
310-393-5593
bed linens

RENTALS

Absolute Party Rental
836 Ritchie Highway, Suite 19
Severna Park, MD 21146
410-544-7474

Arizona Tents & Events
1930 North 22nd Avenue
Phoenix, AZ 85009
602-252-8368

Classic Party Rentals
8476 Stellar Drive
Culver City, CA 90232
310-202-0011

Linen Lenders
14722 Oxnard
Van Nuys, CA 91411
818-781-1181

Party Rental Ltd.
888-774-776